Natasha Vizcarra

ROURKE'S **SCHOOL to HOME** CONNECTIONS

BEFORE AND DURING READING ACTIVITIES

Before Reading: *Building Background Knowledge and Vocabulary*

Building background knowledge can help children process new information and build upon what they already know. Before reading a book, it is important to tap into what children already know about the topic. This will help them develop their vocabulary and increase their reading comprehension.

Questions and Activities to Build Background Knowledge:

1. Look at the front cover of the book and read the title. What do you think this book will be about?
2. What do you already know about this topic?
3. Take a book walk and skim the pages. Look at the table of contents, photographs, captions, and bold words. Did these text features give you any information or predictions about what you will read in this book?

Vocabulary: *Vocabulary Is Key to Reading Comprehension*

Use the following directions to prompt a conversation about each word.

- Read the vocabulary words.
- What comes to mind when you see each word?
- What do you think each word means?

Vocabulary Words:

- *carnivorous*
- *chlorophyll*
- *ecosystems*
- *evolved*
- *nutrients*
- *parasitic*
- *photosynthesis*
- *pollinate*
- *prey*
- *species*

During Reading: *Reading for Meaning and Understanding*

To achieve deep comprehension of a book, children are encouraged to use close reading strategies. During reading, it is important to have children stop and make connections. These connections result in deeper analysis and understanding of a book.

Close Reading a Text

During reading, have children stop and talk about the following:

- Any confusing parts
- Any unknown words
- Text to text, text to self, text to world connections
- The main idea in each chapter or heading

These strategies will help children learn to analyze the text more thoroughly as they read.

When you are finished reading this book, turn to the next-to-last page for **Text-Dependent Questions** and an **Extension Activity**.

Table of Contents

A Most Wonderful Plant!

Ask anyone to describe a plant and they'll probably tell you that it's green, it has leaves, stems, and roots, it loves the sun, and it grows in soil. They might say that big plants are called trees. These are all correct! But did you know that there are weird plants that break the rules of what we think normal plants should be like?

British biologist Charles Darwin was fascinated by these rule-breaking plants. In 1860, Darwin studied sundews and Venus flytraps. These little plants catch and eat insects! He wrote in a letter to a friend that the Venus flytrap is one of "the most wonderful plants in the world."

What makes these plants so fascinating? What are they like? And how did they become so weird? Read on to learn more about these plants that break the rules of nature.

Scientific illustration of a sundew

Plants That Eat Animals

RULE:

PLANTS NEED WATER, SUNLIGHT, AND SOIL NUTRIENTS TO MAKE THEIR FOOD.

Some plants feed on animals like insects, salamanders, and small frogs. These are called **carnivorous** plants. They have clever ways to trap unlucky little critters. The bladderwort's pouches open like trap doors when water flies swim by. This aquatic plant can suck in **prey** in less than one millisecond!

The bladderwort grows floaters to send its yellow flowers above the water.

BLADDERWORT

THE RULE BREAKERS:

BLADDERWORT, BUTTERWORT, PITCHER PLANT, SUNDEW, VENUS FLYTRAP, WATERWHEEL PLANT

BUTTERWORT

Butterworts and sundews have tiny hairs covered in sticky goo. Insects can't resist the sweet nectar on these parts. Once the plants snag a prey, they secrete chemicals to dissolve it. Then they absorb the insect goo as food.

SUNDEW

Pitcher plants release a nectar-like scent to attract prey. Critters crawl into their "pitchers" looking for food. But the plant's waxy walls keep the prey from crawling out. The insect is turned into tasty goo.

Nature's Mouse Trap

The Rajah is the largest pitcher plant in the world. It can grow up to 4 feet (1.2 meters) tall and can digest mice! This **species** is found only in Malaysia.

The Venus flytrap attracts insects with a fruity scent. When a bug lands on its leaves, it triggers sensitive little hairs. The leaves snap shut, trapping the bug in a cage of teeth. Digestive juices dissolve the poor bug.

The waterwheel plant is the underwater version of the Venus flytrap. This plant has about 100 traps. Each trap is 0.08 to 0.16 inches (2 to 4 millimeters) long. The traps may be tiny, but they can catch insects, small fish, and tadpoles.

A Venus flytrap only eats live prey. When it catches something that doesn't move, it opens its trap.

Most plants use their roots to get **nutrients** from soil. Carnivorous plants grow in swamps, bogs, and poor soil. These places lack nutrients. Scientists think the plants **evolved** to eat animals to survive. This took around 140 million years! Insects and small critters are packed with protein and other nutrients. A Venus flytrap can live for three weeks on one large bug.

Meat-eating plants don't eat *all* bugs. They leave bugs alone that **pollinate** their flowers.

A pitcher plant can live for 50 years.

Leaves That Shun the Sun

RULE:

PLANTS NEED SUNLIGHT.

THE KNOWN OFFENDERS:

GHOST PLANT, SNOW PLANT, WOODLAND PINEDROP

These plants don't rely on the sun for energy like many plants do. They don't do **photosynthesis**. Instead, they take energy from fungi that have roots in the soil. Fungi take nutrients from soil and pass them on to trees. Then the trees give fungi carbon, carbohydrates, and other nutrients. Most of these plants are not green. This means they have very little or no **chlorophyll** at all.

GHOST PLANT

Shade-loving plants grow in dark, moist areas in old forests. The ghostly-white ghost plant grows in North and South America and in Asia. The blood-red snow plant lives in the high-elevation forests of California, Nevada, and Oregon. Woodland pinedrops grow in pine forests in North America. They are purple with white, urn-shaped flowers.

Deer like snacking on the woodland pinedrop's tender flowers.

A long time ago, these plants used photosynthesis for energy. But over time they became dependent on fungi, like mushrooms. They lost the ability to make chlorophyll. How this happened is still a mystery to scientists.

Fungi Aren't Plants

Fungi don't use photosynthesis to make their own food. Instead, they live off decaying matter like wood and leaves. Yeast, mold, and mushrooms are examples of fungi.

Plants That Steal

RULE:

PLANTS MAKE THEIR OWN FOOD.

Parasitic plants steal energy to survive. Some survive without their host plants. Some can't. Some end up killing their hosts! Parasitic plants have sneaky ways to suck energy from other plants. Some, like the Australian Christmas tree and the dodder, grow root-like feeding tubes, called haustoria. These poke into their host tree, sucking out water and nutrients.

AUSTRALIAN CHRISTMAS TREE

DODDER

THE DEVIANTS:

AUSTRALIAN CHRISTMAS TREE, CORPSE FLOWER, DODDER, DWARF MISTLETOE, STRANGLER FIG, THURBER'S STEMSUCKER

DWARF MISTLETOE

Some, like the dwarf mistletoe and Thurber's stemsucker, grow on branches like an infection. And then there is the corpse flower. It grows inside its host! Meanwhile, the strangler fig starts its life perched on its host plant. The fig's roots wind around its host as they grow. After reaching soil, its roots thicken. They wrap around the host, stealing its soil and nutrients. Eventually the strangler fig grows so big and tight around its host that it kills it.

THURBER'S STEMSUCKER

STRANGLER FIG

A parasitic plant will always target the same type of host. The strangler fig, for example, really likes cabbage palms. The corpse flower only grows from the tetrastigma vine. How do these plants find their favorites? Scientists have learned that parasitic roots recognize their targets. Their hosts secrete unique chemicals that the parasites remember over many, many generations.

The corpse lily (left) mimics the appearance and smell of dead animals to attract bugs. The titan arum (above), another corpse flower, only blooms every four to ten years.

Leaves That Snap, Leaves That Dance

RULE:

PLANTS DON'T MOVE ON THEIR OWN.

NONCONFORMISTS:

BLADDERWORT, SENSITIVE PLANT, TELEGRAPH PLANT, VENUS FLYTRAP, WATERWHEEL PLANT

Some plants move to follow the sun, but it's slow enough that you can't see it happening. Other plants move right before your eyes! Some, like the sensitive plant, have a kind of plant motor in their stems. These motors use water pressure to puff or deflate its leaves.

The telegraph plant's movement looks a lot like the tapping on the telegraph machine used for Morse code. This is how it got its name.

The telegraph plant seems to move to fool predators. Its leaves wave in circles when exposed to warmth, sunlight, or even loud sounds. It looks like the plant is dancing! Some scientists believe the movement deters butterflies from laying eggs on it—future caterpillars that would munch on its precious leaves.

The sensitive plant's leaves fold shut and its stem droops down when you touch it. Vibrations from the ground or a strong breeze will also cause the plant to fold. Scientists believe this is a protective strategy. It's meant to spook animals grazing nearby.

The sensitive plant is found in Central and South America and Southeast Asia.

The Venus flytrap is a meat eater, and it's also a fast mover. Its leaves snap shut to capture prey. Two other carnivorous plants move fast too. The bladderwort's hollow sacs suck insects in. The waterwheel's trap has hinged jaws, like the Venus flytrap. These plants all have tiny hairs that trigger the trap when stepped on by little insect legs.

BLADDERWORT

Who's the Fastest?

These snap-trappers and dancers move all on their own.
But some are faster than others.

Fastest Trap Shutters

BLADDERWORT:
SHUTS ITS TRAP IN
0.0052 TO 0.1 SECONDS

WATERWHEEL:
SHUTS ITS TRAP IN
0.01 TO 0.1 SECONDS

VENUS FLYTRAP:
SHUTS ITS TRAP IN
0.1 TO 0.3 SECONDS

Slowpokes

SENSITIVE PLANT:
FOLDS ITS LEAVES IN
4 TO 5 SECONDS

TELEGRAPH PLANT:
WAVES ITS LEAVES
IN A CIRCLE IN
90 SECONDS

Scientists are fascinated by these fast-moving plants. Charles Darwin even wondered if they were animals. Scientists have decided that they are indeed plants. They believe these plants' ancestors evolved to respond quickly to threats around them. That took hundreds of years. How did they learn to move? That remains a mystery.

Scientists love to study such cool plants, like this Venus flytrap.

Fruits That Explode

RULE:

FRUITS JUST FALL FROM TREES.

Most plants spread their seeds by dropping their fruit. Some seeds have fuzz or wings to travel by wind. Others grow spikes and hitch rides on animals. But some plants get their fruit to explode! The sandbox tree in North and South America is the most explosive. When its fruits ripen, they explode with a force that shoots seeds a distance of 147 feet (44.81 meters). That's about the length of two tennis courts.

The Sound of Fruit

The sandbox tree fruit is called Monkey's Dinner Bell in Brazil. When monkeys hear the fruits explode, they rush to eat it.

SANDBOX TREE

PUNKS:

HAIRY BITTERCRESS, MEDITERRANEAN SQUIRTING CUCUMBER, ORANGE JEWELWEED, SANDBOX TREE

The Mediterranean squirting cucumber is just as scary. When its fruits fall from their stems, they shoot goo-covered seeds 10 to 20 feet (3 to 6 meters) away. The goo is toxic to humans and animals. The orange jewelweed is called touch-me-not for a good reason. When lightly touched, its pods shoot seeds as far as 4 to 6 feet (1.2 to 1.8 meters). The hairy bittercress flings its seeds 16 feet (4.88 meters) away. This startles insects and birds that want to snack on the seeds.

Dangerous Seeds

The seeds of the sandbox tree fruit can reach a velocity of 229 feet (69.80 meters) per second. That's much faster than an average major league fastball pitch of 140 feet (42.67 meters) per sccond.

How do these fruits explode? Many of the fruits use stored elastic energy. Think of the tension that builds in a slingshot as you pull on the elastic. When you let go of the elastic, this tension releases with great force. In the sandbox tree fruit, the tension in the seed pods increases as the fruit dries. It's released when the pods break open.

Plants That Love Fire

RULE:

FIRE KILLS PLANTS.

REBELS:

AUSTRALIAN GRASS TREE, BANKSIA, BUCKBRUSH, EUCALYPTUS, FIRE LILY, LODGEPOLE PINE

Fires turn trees and plants to ashes. But did you know that there are plants that *need* fire to survive? Some, like the eucalyptus, banksia, buckbrush, and lodgepole pine, have fire-activated seeds. Their cones and fruits are covered with a special resin. Only the heat of a wildfire or bushfire can melt this covering. A year after a fire, the burnt remains of an old tree can be found surrounded by its new saplings.

EUCALYPTUS

BANKSIA

Some plants can resprout quickly after being damaged by fire. Some types of eucalyptus have special buds under their bark. Fire causes these buds to sprout. They quickly grow into new leaves and branches after a fire. The banksia has fat bottom stems. They also sprout new shoots after a fire. The fire lily in South Africa blooms only after a smoky fire.

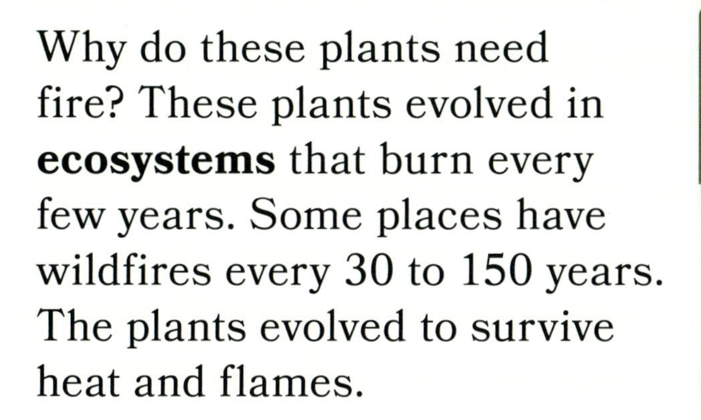

Why do these plants need fire? These plants evolved in **ecosystems** that burn every few years. Some places have wildfires every 30 to 150 years. The plants evolved to survive heat and flames.

Can't Catch Me!

The lodgepole pine drops off its lower branches as the tree grows taller. This prevents fire from climbing up to its flammable canopy.

Hot, dry climates make the Australian outback (above) and the San Gabriel Mountains in the US (right) prone to wildfires.

Plants That Have Lots to Teach

Today's scientists continue to be fascinated by these rule-breaking plants. We have a lot to learn from them. Researchers think the Venus flytrap holds the key to building soft robots. Doctors think the sundew's sticky goo can help them develop better medical adhesives to heal wounds. The list goes on!

SUNDEW

If you think about it, these strange plants are cool! And they are problem solvers. Live in a bog with no soil nutrients? Eat flies. Live in a place that keeps burning? Use the fire to survive. How cool is that?

Glossary

carnivorous (kahr-NIV-ur-uhs): having meat as a regular part of the diet

chlorophyll (KLOR-uh-fil): the green substance in plants that uses light to manufacture food from carbon dioxide and water

ecosystems (EE-koh-sis-tuhmz): all the living things in a place and their relation to their environment

evolved (i-VAHLVD): to have changed slowly and naturally over time

nutrients (NOO-tree-uhnts): substances such as proteins, minerals, or vitamins that are needed by plants to stay strong and healthy

parasitic (par-uh-SIT-ik): living on or inside another plant

photosynthesis (foh-toh-SIN-thi-sis): a chemical process by which green plants and some other organisms make their food

pollinate (PAH-luh-nate): to carry or transfer pollen from the stamen to the pistil of the same flower or another flower where female cells can be fertilized to produce seed

prey (pray): an animal taken by a predator as food

species (SPEE-sheez): one of the groups into which plants of the same genus are divided

Index

Text-Dependent Questions

1. Name the famous biologist who was fascinated by carnivorous plants.
2. Why do carnivorous plants eat insects and other small animals?
3. When does the fruit of a sandbox tree explode?
4. What do you call a plant that depends on another plant for energy and food?
5. Where would you find plants that need fire to survive?

Extension Activity

Before photography was invented, people made drawings of plants they saw in nature. Charles Darwin was an excellent botanical artist! You can experience what it's like to be a botanical artist by observing house plants in your home. Or visit a local botanical garden with an adult. Try to find one of the plants in this book, like the Venus flytrap. Observe the plant and draw it in a notebook. Label the parts. Write down other observations at the bottom of the drawing. Write down a few unanswered questions you have about it too.

About the Author

Natasha Vizcarra is a science writer and an award-winning children's book author. She grew up in the Philippines where the sensitive plant grows everywhere. Filipinos call it "makahiya," meaning "shy plant." Learn more about Natasha and her books at www.natashavizcarra.com.

www.rourkebooks.com

PHOTO CREDITS: Cover: ©EsHanPhot/Shutterstock, ©Romolo Tavani/Shutterstock, ©Cavan-Images/Shutterstock, ©Julian Popov/Shutterstock, ©Reongshewa/Shutterstock; page 3: ©New Africa/Shutterstock, ©William Cushman/Shutterstock: pages 4–32: ©New Africa/Shutterstock; page 4: ©William Cushman/Shutterstock, ©Gene and Muyu/Shutterstock, ©Sarka Stuchlikova/Shutterstock; page 5: ©Little daisy/Shutterstock, ©Nicku/Shutterstock, ©Morphart Creation/Shutterstock; page 6: ©D. Kucharski K. Kucharska/Shutterstock, ©F_studio/Shutterstock; page 7: ©Little daisy/Shutterstock, ©ArikEkaSatya/Shutterstock, ©Lubomir Dajc/Shutterstock, ©Chainarong Phrammanee/Shutterstock; page 8: ©DMVPhotography/Getty Images, ©Kouzou Yoneyama/Getty Images, ©Kuttelvaserova Stuchelova/Shutterstock; page 9: ©Sarka Stuchlikova/Shutterstock, ©Marina Kryuchina/Shutterstock; page 10: ©Clyde Sorenson, CC BY-ND, ©hwongcc/Shutterstock, ©Cavan-Images/Shutterstock; pages 11–13: ©merrymuuu/Shutterstock; page 12: ©William Cushman/Shutterstock, ©Gene and Muyu/Shutterstock; page 13: ©Bukhta Yurii/Shutterstock, ©Rebecca Doherty/Shutterstock; page 14: ©KarenHBlack/Shutterstock, ©Hans Wismeijer/Shutterstock; page 15: ©2020 Matt Berger, ©TamuT/Shutterstock, ©IvanaStevanoski/Shutterstock; page 16: ©AwakeTaH/Shutterstock, ©irin-k/Shutterstock, ©Mazur Travel/Shutterstock, ©Bpk Maizal/Shutterstock; page 17: ©Gheorghe Mindru/Shutterstock; page 18: ©AjayTvm/Shutterstock; page 19: ©Kouzou Yoneyama/Getty Images, ©D. Kucharski K. Kucharska/Shutterstock; page 20: ©Kouzou Yoneyama/Getty Images, ©Jeff Holcombe/Shutterstock, ©MakroBetz/Shutterstock, ©Three Babies Images/Shutterstock, ©Dendy12/Shutterstock; page 21: ©AndreyUG/Shutterstock; page 22: ©Estefan_D/Shutterstock, ©zaidiamri/Shutterstock; page 23: ©Julian Popov/Shutterstock, ©MLHoward/Shutterstock, ©Nimrod Abella/Shutterstock, ©vandycan/Shutterstock, ©MVelishchuk/Shutterstock; page 24: ©Ljupco Smokovski/Shutterstoc, ©Nahhana/Shutterstock, ©Michael Kraus/Shutterstock; pages 25–27: ©james benjamin/Shutterstock; page 25: ©Bildagentur Zoonar GmbH/Shutterstock, ©Daria Nipot/Shutterstock; page 26: ©Reongshewa/Shutterstock, ©Daria Nipot/Shutterstock; page 27: ©VD Image Lab/Shutterstock, ©Sara Kendall/Shutterstock, ©photojohn830/Shutterstock; page 28: ©thecloudysunny/Shutterstock, ©PeopleImages.com - Yuri A/Shutterstock; page 29: ©Ernie Cooper/Shutterstock, ©Dolores M. Harvey/Shutterstock, ©Ekaterina Verbis/Shutterstock, ©KarenHBlack/Shutterstock

Quote source (page 5): Thomas C. Gibson and Donald M. Waller, "Evolving Darwin's 'Most Wonderful' Plant: Ecological Steps to a Snap-Trap," New Phytologist 183, no. 3 (2009): 575–87, https://doi.org/10.1111/j.1469-8137.2009.02935.x.

Edited by: Catherine Malaski
Cover and interior layout by: Nick Pearson

Library of Congress PCN Data

Plants That Break the Rules / Natasha Vizcarra
(Nature's Rule Breakers)
ISBN 978-1-73165-801-2 (hard cover)
ISBN 978-1-73165-807-4 (soft cover)
ISBN 978-1-73165-813-5 (e-book)
ISBN 978-1-73165-819-7 (e-pub)
Library of Congress Control Number: 2024932717

Rourke Educational Media
Printed in the United States of America
02-3042411937